DEDICATION

To the Husband, the Little Guy, Little Bean, and Mom. You all mean more to me than words can express.

table of contents

Introduction

I was the oldest of a single-parent family. Mom worked full time while attending night classes, and making dinner was an easy way for me to help.

I remember roasting chicken legs, boiling water for pasta and cooking pizza for my little brother after school. It was fun. I never look at cooking as a job or a chore and neither did Mom. I have fond memories of cooking with her, talking over a pot of spaghetti sauce or baking holiday cookies.

Cookers are normally eaters. I wasn't a very thin adolescent, which was nicely pointed out to me on many occasions by my father and classmates. **By the age of 12, I was already uncomfortable in my own skin.**

Throughout high school and college I consistently gained and lost the 10 pounds, which turned into the same 20 then 30, 40 … you get the idea. This cycle continued until I had my first child.

Having my son changed my life drastically. Of course there were sleepless nights and diapers, but **he also gave me a new perspective and lust for life.** It was more than just about me now. I had to get over the bad body image and extreme yo-yo dieting. I had to learn how to eat healthy and be healthy, so I could teach my little guy good habits.

Over the next year I overhauled my entire diet and approach to food. **I blogged about my weight loss. I shared ideas online. I became 70 pounds lighter!** It really wasn't a miracle, although it sure felt like one. I actually now weigh less than that young insecure girl who helped her mom make dinner.

It's been over five years since losing the weight, and a huge part of my success has been preparing my own food. I may not be a trained chef or professional cook but since I've never been afraid of the kitchen, I experiment. I enjoy the challenge of lightening up a dish or finding a way to make a fun, non-traditional dessert. **I'm a big believer in "everything in moderation,"** but when you like to eat as much as I do, keeping my meals as light as possible helps keep my weight in a healthy range.

My Approach to lighter cooking

My personality, interest, and motivation for lighter meals are what drive me. So much of what I do in the kitchen comes from experimentation.

My mission is simple: Fast, family-friendly food that uses lots of fruits and vegetables while keeping sugar, refined carbs and fat at a minimum. I'm not making any claims to low-fat, low-carb, high-fiber or any other craze that struck us over the past few years. **I'm talking food, mostly unprocessed whole food with an eye on convenience.** It's all about balance, and I hope my ideas spark some of your own.

Take the ideas in this book and make them your own. Add your spin. Replace things your family doesn't like. Try a different cooking technique. **Just lose the fear of the kitchen** and own what you are putting in you and your family's bodies.

Cooking and eating should be enjoyable. In today's world we've grown so accustomed to convenience food that we forget how much fun it can be -- especially when you have kids. **Family time over a meal is wonderful. Family time while cooking that meal is even better!**

My Pantry

I consider myself very much a pantry cook. I rarely, if ever, find a recipe, go out and buy all the ingredients and then make a meal. Instead, I stock my home with ingredients I can easily use to whip up dinner.

Canned foods: I always have a plethora of canned goods in my pantry. I stock up when things are on sale and hit the wholesale clubs when I get a chance. My must-haves include:

- Diced tomatoes
- Tomato sauce
- Crushed tomatoes
- Tomato paste
- Fruit (pineapple, Mandarin oranges, anything in its own juice or light syrup)
- Corn
- Green beans
- Beans (black, Northern, pinto, garbanzo)
- Tuna
- Low-sodium/Healthy Request creamed soups

My Pantry (continued)

Grains, pastas and cereals: From baking and breakfast to side dishes and salads, having a variety of grains and cereals gives me a lot of options when I'm contemplating what to cook.

- Whole wheat flour
- White whole wheat flour
- Bulgur
- Wheat bran
- Quinoa
- Brown rice (instant and dried)
- Whole wheat couscous
- Whole wheat pasta (variety of shapes and sizes)
- Rolled oats
- Steel-cut oats
- High-fiber, low-sugar cereals (Fiber One, All-Bran, Grape-Nuts)

Spices and condiments: The spice cabinet is the center of my kitchen. Without it I am crippled, but stocking it can get awfully expensive. I always walk by the spice aisle in the grocery store and buy anything on sale even if I don't know how to use it or need it at the moment.

I also buy the cheap or no-name brand of the basics (garlic powder, onion powder, parsley, basil, oregano, chili powder) whenever I can. With these base spices you have a good starting point for a lot of quick dishes.

Other things found in my spice cabinet:

- Honey
- Worcestershire sauce
- Soy sauce
- Vinegars (white, apple, red wine, rice)
- Oils (olive, sesame, canola)
- Baking soda
- Baking powder
- Mini chocolate chips
- Sprinkles (they make everything better)
- Kosher salt
- Non-stick spray (olive and canola variety)

The freezer: I always try to keep the following items just a defrost away:

- Bags of frozen vegetables (broccoli, sugar snap peas, stir-fry mixes)
- Bags of frozen fruits (strawberries, wild blueberries, mixed berries)
- Ground meats frozen in 1-pound bags (lean beef, lean turkey)
  Thin-cut pork chops
  Boneless chicken breasts
- Whole chicken (approximately 3-4 pounds)
- Pork tenderloin
- Turkey tenderloin

All recipes in this book come from GreenLiteBites.com. I continue to post new ideas and tips there as well as modify and update older ones.

For more nutritional information, supporting videos, additional photos and updates on any recipes printed in this book, visit the companion site, **GreenLiteBites.com/thebook**

You can also find me online at my other blogs:

Roni's Weigh (RonisWeigh.com)
RoniNoone.com (RoniNoone.com)
BlogToLose (BlogToLose.com)
SkinnyMinnyMedia (SkinnyMinnyMedia.com)
If you twitter I'm @RoniNoone. Feel free to say hi!

Special Thanks to the Editor: Gail Gedan Spencer
Photographs by: Roni Noone

Special Thanks to High5Design:
David Zobel: Creative Director
Lee Morton: Art Director
Colleen Campbell: Designer
Devin McCurley: Designer

Illustrations by: David Zobel
http://www.high5design.net

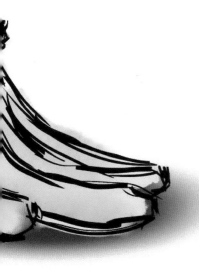

Breakfast

GreenLightBites

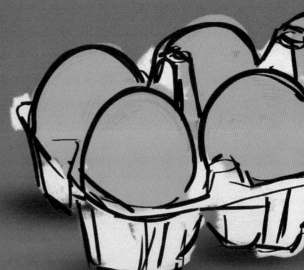

This is a family favorite of ours! The pancakes go wonderfully with traditional maple syrup but even better dipped in unsweetened applesauce or smeared with a bit of low-sugar strawberry jelly.

whole multi-grain pancakes

STEPS

1. **In a medium bowl,** combine oats, milk and lemon juice. Let the mixture sit while preparing the dry ingredients (at least 2 minutes).

2. In another bowl, **combine the rest** of the dry ingredients. Set aside.

3. **Beat or whisk the egg,** vanilla, applesauce and honey into the milk/oatmeal mixture. It will be very runny.

4. **Add the dry ingredients** to the wet and mix with a spoon until just combined.

5. **Pour between 1/8 and 1/4 cup of the batter** on a non-stick skillet or griddle over medium heat sprayed with non-stick cooking spray. Cook about 1-2 minutes a side; small bubbles will form but not as many as traditional pancakes. Just peek underneath for a light brown color, then flip.

INGREDIENTS

- 1/2 cup quick or rolled oats (40g)
- 1 cup skim milk (8 oz)
- 2 tsp lemon juice
- 3/4 cup whole wheat flour (90g)
- 1 tsp cinnamon
- 1/2 tsp nutmeg
- 1/2 tsp baking soda
- 1/2 tsp baking powder
- 1 egg
- 1 tsp vanilla
- 1 tbsp unsweetened applesauce (optional)
- 1 tbsp honey
- Non-stick cooking spray

OUT OF MILK?
Replace with 1/4 cup nonfat yogurt and 1/4 cup water.

WANT WAFFLES?
Use the batter in your waffle iron!

HAVE BLUEBERRIES?
Add them to the batter. This makes a great blueberry pancake!

1 serving, 100 cals, 0g ot tat, 3g ot tiber.

green tea & tropical fruit smoothie

INGREDIENTS

- 1 mango-flavored green tea bag
- 4 oz boiling water
- Ice cubes
- 1/3 cup fresh pineapple, cut in chunks (70g)
- 1/2 banana
- 1/3 cup fresh papaya, cut in chunks (40g)

NOT A TROPICAL FRUIT FAN?
Try the same technique with berries and a peach-flavored green tea.

WORRIED ABOUT CAFFEINE?
Use decaf!

NO FRESH PINEAPPLE?
Canned would work great, too!

STEPS

1. Brew the tea with the 4 oz of water.

2. Let the tea bag steep for at least 2 minutes and then fill the tea cup with about 5 ice cubes to cool it down.

3. Add the cooled tea, a few more ice cubes and fruit in the blender. Blend until smooth

Here's a refreshing smoothie that replaces the traditional milk or yogurt with brewed green tea. The result is a light, tasty breakfast on the go!

spinach egg muffins

About 2 servings, 100 cals, 7g of fat, 1g of fiber.

STEPS

1. **Preheat the oven** to 375 degrees.

2. **Whisk the eggs** and spinach with a pinch of salt and pepper.

3. **Spray a mini-muffin pan** with non-stick cooking spray. Using a tablespoon, dollop the egg-spinach mixture unto eight mini-muffins.

4. **Sprinkle Parmesan cheese** and bacon bits on top and bake for 10-12 minutes.

INGREDIENTS

- 2 eggs
- 1 cup baby spinach, chopped
- 1 tbsp (7g) real bacon bits
- 1 tbsp (5g) grated parmesan cheese
- Non-stick cooking spray
- Kosher salt and pepper

Here's a spin on morning eggs that is fun for adults and kids alike. They are great dipped in ketchup!

DON'T LIKE SPINACH?

Replace with diced onion, pepper and ham for a Western omelet twist.

EGG MUFFINS STICKING?

Try a silicone muffin pan.

WANT MORE WHILE KEEPING IT LIGHT?

Add a few egg whites.

apple pie oatmeal

1 serving, 210 cals, 3g of fat, 7g of fiber.

STEPS

1. **Put the oats,** water, sweetener and cinnamon in a small pot over medium-high heat. Cook and stir until water is absorbed, about 5 minutes.

2. **Mix the cooked oatmeal** with applesauce. Sprinkle with additional cinnamon.

INGREDIENTS

- 1/2 cup (40g) rolled oats
- 6 oz water
- 1 packet sweetener (like Truvia)
- 1 tsp ground cinnamon
- 1/2 cup unsweetened applesauce

DON'T HAVE SWEETENER?
Try a tablespoon of honey.

NO ROLLED OATS?
Use quick or instant.

LIKE IT CREAMIER?
Add a dollop of non-fat vanilla yogurt!

It's so fast and so yummy, you will never buy prepackaged flavored oatmeal again!

whole wheat blueberry pancake waffles

About 4 servings, 175 cals, 3g of fat, 5g of fiber.

INGREDIENTS

- 1 cup white whole wheat flour (120g)
- 1 tsp cinnamon
- 1/2 tsp baking soda
- 1/2 tsp baking powder
- 1 cup almond milk (8 oz) (could use fat-free milk)
- 1 egg
- 1 tsp vanilla
- 1/4 cup unsweetened applesauce (61g)
- 1 tbsp honey (21g)
- 1/2 cup blueberries (74g)

STEPS

1. **Mix the flour,** cinnamon, baking soda and baking powder together in a small bowl and set aside. Use a fork or whisk to help aerate it a bit.

2. In another bowl, **whisk the milk,** egg, vanilla, applesauce and honey until frothy. Add the blueberries.

3. **Pour the flour mixture** into the milk mixture and continue to fold until just combined. Don't overmix.

4. **Add the batter** to your skillet or waffle iron sprayed with non-stick spray.

Waffles? Pancakes? It's all the same batter to me. This recipe works great for either.

DON'T HAVE FRESH BLUEBERRIES?

Frozen work great, too, especially the small, wild ones.

WANT TO CHANGE UP THE FLAVORS?

Skip the applesauce and add a mashed ripe banana with some chocolate chips!

WAFFLES COMING OUT TOO SOFT?

Cook an extra minute or two to help crisp them.

strawberry papaya smoothie

1 serving, 105 cals, 0g of fat, 3g of fiber.

INGREDIENTS

- 1 cup papaya, cut in chunks (140 g)
- 1/4 cup non-fat unsweetened yogurt (60g)
- 4 large frozen strawberries

STEPS

1. **Blend and serve!**

2. **The top-down approach** using a hand blender works best. If you use a traditional blender, you may need to add additional liquid like water or apple juice.

A light, nutritious breakfast you can drink on the go. This idea is simple, tasty and requires no additional sweetener or sugar. The strawberries and papaya are a great combination!

PAPAYA TOO BIG FOR JUST ONE SMOOTHIE?
Buy it then freeze leftovers in 1-cup portions

HAVE FRESH STRAWBERRIES?
Use them instead and add a couple of ice cubes.

LIKE IT SWEETER?
Replace the unsweetened yogurt with your favorite flavored light yogurt cup.

100% whole wheat
banana muffins

About 6 servings, 250 cals, 4g of fat, 7g of fiber.

STEPS

1. **Preheat the oven** to 375 degrees.

2. **Mix and double sift** the whole wheat flour, baking soda, baking powder and salt. Set aside

3. In a medium bowl, **mash the banana** with a fork. Add the egg whites, yogurt, honey, molasses, applesauce and extract. Whisk until well blended and a bit frothy.

4. **Mix the sifted flour** with the banana-egg mixture until just moistened. Don't overmix!

5. **Spray a six-muffin pan** with non-stick cooking spray.

6. **Evenly distribute the batter** in the muffin tin cups. Sprinkle with rolled oats. Bake for about 18 minutes.

INGREDIENTS

- 11/4 cups (150g) whole wheat flour
- 1/2 tsp baking soda
- 1/2 tsp baking powder
- 1/4 tsp salt
- 1 large overripe banana
- 2 egg whites
- 1/2 cup plain non-fat yogurt
- 1 tbsp honey (21g)
- 1 tbsp molasses (20g)
- 1/4 cup applesauce
- 1 tsp almond extract
- 1 tbsp rolled oats

HAVE FUN WITH THE KIDS!
Let them add sprinkles instead of the oats.

CHANGE IT UP!
Add some cinnamon and blueberries!

LIKE CRUNCH?
Add some chopped almonds or walnuts!

The result of quite a few experiments, this banana muffin recipe is a favorite in our house.

Oatmeal on the go, how can you go wrong? Add some ripe bananas and mini chocolate chips and you have a family favorite.

banana oatmeal cups

STEPS

1. Preheat oven to 375 degrees.

2. Mix all ingredients except the chocolate chips, & let sit for at least 10 minutes while you prepare the muffin pans.

3. Place 15 liners in two muffin pans. Spray with a bit of non-stick spray.

4. Stir the chocolate chips into the oatmeal batter.

5. Divide batter into 15 muffin cups. They should be just about filled.

6. Bake 20-30 minutes; you'll see the edges just starting to brown and they will be firm to the touch.

7. The muffins may stick when hot but are removed easily when cooled. Aluminum liners work best!

INGREDIENTS

- 3 overripe bananas, mashed
- 1 cup skim milk or light vanilla soy or almond milk
- 2 eggs
- 1 tbsp baking powder
- 3 cups (240g) rolled oats
- 1 tsp vanilla extract
- 3 tbsp (42g) mini chocolate chips
- Non-stick cooking spray

15 MUFFINS TOO MANY?
Freeze the leftovers and pop into the microwave for a quick breakfast.

NO CHOCOLATE CHIPS?
Replace with some frozen berries!

ONLY TWO BANANAS?
Replace the missing one with 1/2 cup unsweetened applesauce.

GreenLiteBites

Lunch

Who says you need sauce and dough for pizza? This is a fun, fast twist for my fellow pizza addicts out there.

mexican pizza

INGREDIENTS

- 1 whole wheat/low-carb tortilla
- 1/4 cup fat free refried beans (60g)
- 2 tbsp of your favorite salsa (30g)
- Pinch of kosher salt
- About 1/4 cup diced peppers
  (I used a mix of red and green)
- 1 oz fancy shredded Mexican cheese blend
- Sprinkle of chili powder and dried cilantro

STEPS

1. **Preheat oven** to 425 degrees.

2. **Pierce the tortilla** with a knife a few times and bake until crispy and the ends just start to brown. Time will vary based on size.

3. **Mix the beans,** salsa and salt together. Smear it on the tortilla. Top with the peppers and cheese. Bake for about 5 minutes.

4. After pulling it out of the oven, **sprinkle with chili** powder and cilantro.

LIKE IT HOT?
Add a diced hot pepper or use spicy salsa!

NO REFRIED BEANS?
Use tomato paste instead, skip the salsa and spice it up with chili powder, cumin and kosher salt.

CAN'T FIND WHOLE WHEAT TORTILLAS?
Use flatbread, naan, lavash or any other thin whole-grain bread product.

1 serving, 220 cals, 9g of fat, 7g of fiber.

STEPS

1. **Wash and prepare** all your ingredients.

2. Top the greens with the berries and cheese. **Drizzle on the dressing** and enjoy!

INGREDIENTS

- 3-4 cups of fresh romaine lettuce, cleaned and torn
- About 1/2 cup fresh blueberries
- About 1/2 cup fresh strawberries, cut in small chunks
- 1 oz (28g) crumbled feta
- 1 tbsp poppyseed dressing

red, white & blue sweet summer salad

CAN'T FIND POPPYSEED DRESSING?

Try another sweet option like French, Vidalia onion or even honey mustard!

DON'T LIKE FETA?

Try this salad with cottage instead or even shredded Parmesan.

DON'T WANT TO BUY A HEAD OF LETTUCE?

The bagged stuff works great! Use the leftovers for taco night!

Sometimes simple things make the best quick meals. The combo of fresh berries, lettuce and a sweet dressing with a salty cheese is a real treat and a totally satisfying lunch!

sandwich sushi

1 serving, 165 cals, 4g of fat, 4g of fiber.

INGREDIENTS

- 1 spreadable light cheese wedge
- Squirt of honey mustard
- 1/2 slice of Lavash or flatbread
- 3 slices of thin-sliced turkey breast
- 1 slice thin-sliced lean ham
- 3 slices of turkey pepperoni
- 5-6 baby spinach leaves, stems removed
- 2 baby carrots, grated

STEPS

1. **Smear the cheese** and mustard on the bread. Start layering the ingredients as seen in the pictures. Leave about 2 inches on the end; as you roll the fillings will squish outward.

2. Roll as tightly as you can. **Cut with a serrated knife** as to not squish.

DON'T LIKE HONEY MUSTARD?
Use dijon, brown or yellow.

NO TURKEY PEPPERONI?
Skip it, AND add an extra slice of ham.

WANT MORE CRUNCH?
Add julienned cucumber or carrots, just like traditional sushi.

I initially came up with this idea for the toddler who declared he "didn't like sandwiches!" Well, to my surprise, I now eat Sandwich Sushi fairly regularly. The toddler? A sandwich. Go figure.

25

southwest
turkey burgers

INGREDIENTS

- 8 oz extra lean ground turkey
- 1/3 of a red bell pepper, diced small
- 1/3 of a green bell pepper, diced small
- 1/3 of a yellow bell pepper, diced small
- 1/2 of a small onion, diced small
- 1 medium button mushroom, diced small (optional)
- 1 egg white
- 1/4 cup quick oats (20g)
- 1 tsp chili powder
- 1/4 tsp red pepper flakes (or to taste)
- 1/2 tsp cumin
- 1 tsp dried cilantro
- Pinch of kosher salt & pepper
- Non-stick cooking spray

STEPS

1. Put all ingredients (except spray) in a bowl and combine with hands.

2. Form the mixture into four equal patties approximately 4 ounces each.

3. Grill about 4-5 minutes a side or about 6 minutes on a table-top grill.

MY FAVORITE WAY TO SERVE?

On a whole wheat roll or english muffin with a bed of baby spinach, tomatoes and ketchup.

DON'T HAVE GROUND TURKEY?

Lean ground beef or chicken work, too!

ONLY HAVE 1 GREEN PEPPER?

Just use the whole thing instead of the red & yellow.

I routinely make a double batch of these and freeze leftovers for a quick lunch. Just pop the patty in the microwave and add it to your favorite whole wheat bun with all the fixin's.

WHAT DO I DO WITH IT?
Stuff it in a pita, roll it in a wrap, top your favorite salad greens!

NO RED ONION?
A sweet onion works great, too!

NO KIDNEY BEANS?
Try black or pinto!

kidney bean & corn salsa salad

Super flavorful, really fast and very versatile! This can quickly be whipped up for lunch, and the leftovers are even better the next day.

INGREDIENTS

- 1 tbsp honey
- 1 tbsp lime juice
- 1 tbsp dried cilantro
- 1 tsp chili powder
- 1/2 tsp ground cumin
- 1 tsp Tabasco sauce (or to taste)
- 1 can (15 oz) red kidney beans, drained and rinsed
- 1 small can (8 oz) sweet yellow corn, drained and rinsed
- 2 -3 slices red onion, diced small

STEPS

1. **Whisk the honey,** lime juice, cilantro, chili powder, cumin and Tabasco sauce in a medium bowl.

2. Add the beans, corn and onion. **Toss and let flavors mix.**

fiesta chicken
salad

1 serving, 210 cals, 4g of fat, 3g of fiber.

STEPS

1. **Put the chicken,** onion, peppers and tomatoes in a medium bowl.

2. In a small bowl, whisk the yogurt, vinegar, jalapeño liquid, lime juice and spices **to make the dressing.**

3. Pour the yogurt dressing over the chicken and veggies. Stir to **coat everything.**

INGREDIENTS

- 8 oz leftover or cooked chicken breast, cubed
- 1/4 cup red onion, diced
- 1 cup diced peppers
- 1/2 jalapeño pepper, diced (from jar) (more or less depending on taste)
- 1 cup tomatoes, diced
- 2 tbsp unsweetened fat-free yogurt
- 1 tbsp red wine vinegar
- 1 tbsp jalapeño liquid from the jar
- Juice of 1/2 lime or about 2 tsp
- 1/2 tsp chili powder
- 1 tsp dried cilantro

Who says you need mayo to make a tasty chicken salad? This idea uses a bit of yogurt, vinegar and jalapeño pepper liquid to make a tasty spicy alternative to traditional chicken salad.

WHAT DO I DO WITH IT?
Stuff a pita, top your favorite salad greens or eat it straight up!

WANT A MORE COLORFUL SALAD?
Use multicolor peppers and exotic tomatoes.

DON'T LIKE IT SPICY?
Skip the jalapeño.

WHAT DO I DO WITH IT?
Stuff a pita!

WHERE DO I GET COOKED CHICKEN?
Make an extra breast next time you cook dinner or buy precooked from the grocery store!

WHAT IF I DON'T LIKE HONEYDEW?
Try cantaloupe or halve some grapes!

Pairing chicken with fruit is not only fun but tasty! Here we tone down the sweetness with tart yogurt and lime juice.

STEPS

1. Mix the yogurt, lime juice and cilantro to make the dressing.

2. Place the chicken, melon, mango and tomatoes in a bowl and toss with the dressing.

INGREDIENTS

- 1/4 cup plain non-fat yogurt (57g)
- Juice of one lime
- 1 tsp dried cilantro
- 8 oz cooked chicken breast
- 1 cup honeydew melon, cubed (170g)
- 1 cup mango, cubed (165g)
- 1 cup grape tomatoes, halved (150g)

sweet
chicken salad

GreenLiteBites

Soups

light lentil soup

5 servings, 150 cals, 2g of fat, 10g of fiber.

INGREDIENTS

- Non-stick cooking spray
- 1 small sweet onion, chopped
- 3 cloves of garlic, minced
- 1 cup fresh carrots, sliced
- 2 tbsp (14g) real bacon bits
- 2 tbsp tomato paste
- 1 cup (128g) dried lentils, rinsed
- 1/2 tsp dried thyme
- 5 cups chicken broth

STEPS

1. Spray medium pot with non-stick cooking spray and warm over medium heat. Add the onion and garlic, cooking for a few minutes until tender.

2. Stir in the carrots and bacon bits.

3. Continue to cook, adding the tomato paste. Stir and coat all the veggies with the paste.

4. Stir in the lentils, thyme and broth.

5. Bring to a boil, stirring occasionally, then reduce to a simmer. Continue to simmer for about an hour.

ONLY BUY BABY CARROTS?
They work great!

HAVE LEFT OVER PORK OR CHICKEN?
Add it in for extra protein and flavor!

TOO MANY SERVINGS?
Freeze the leftovers for lunches in single-serve plastic containers.

Inspired by a traditional lentil soup recipe, this idea uses bacon bits to get the flavor of bacon without all the added fat.

sweet pepper & hot sausage soup

STEPS

1. **Spray a large stock pot** with cooking spray. Add the onion and garlic, cook over medium heat until vegetables get a bit translucent.

2. Remove the casings from the sausage by simply slicing them length-wise. **Add the sausage meat to the pot** and break up while browning. Add the basil, oregano, thyme and parsley and stir.

3. Once the sausage is browned, add the peppers and tomatoes. Add the diced tomatoes, broth and paste. **Stir, bring to a boil and lower to a simmer.** Simmer about 20 minutes until peppers just soften.

NOT A SPICY FAN?
Use sweet Italian sausage instead.

NOT FILLING ENOUGH?
Add some brown rice or bulgur.

CAN'T FIND TURKEY SAUSAGE?
Use ground turkey and spice it up!

INGREDIENTS

- Non-stick cooking spray
- 1 sweet onion, minced
- 6 cloves of garlic minced
- 20 oz package of hot Italian turkey sausage
- 1 tsp dried basil
- 1/2 tsp dried oregano
- 1/2 tsp dried thyme
- 1 tbsp dried parsley
- 3 large multicolored bell peppers, chopped
- 1/2 pint cherry tomatoes, halved
- 1 (15 oz) can diced tomatoes
- 6 cups chicken broth
- 1 (6 oz) can tomato paste

A super flavorful soup that uses the spice of prepackaged Italian sausage & the sweetness of bell peppers. This is fabulous on a cold fall day.

No one will ever guess there's no cream in this creamy soup. The apple gives a slight sweetness, the spices balance it out and the seeds add a nice crunch.

winter squash soup with roasted seeds

STEPS

1. Preheat the oven to 350 degrees.

2. Cut both squash in half, scraping out and saving the seeds.

3. Core the apple. Line a cookie sheet with aluminum foil & spray with non-stick cooking spray. Lay the sqaush flesh side down, place the apple on and bake for 45 minutes to an hour.

4. While the squash is baking, clean the pulp from the seeds, rinse them and allow to dry on a paper towel.

5. Remove squash from the oven and let cool a little.

6. While the squash is cooling line another cookie sheet with aluminum foil and spray with non-stick cooking spray. Lay the seeds out and sprinkle with kosher salt. Bake for about 10-15 minutes until toasted.

7. While the seeds are toasting, add the squash, spices and broth to the blender. You are going to have to do about three batches as it's alot of soup.

8. Continue to simmer until ready to serve.

9. Place two ladlefuls, about 1 cup, in a bowl and sprinkle with about 1 tbsp of the toasted seeds and a pinch of dried parsley. Add the seeds just before eating; they will tenderize in the soup and lose their crunch.

INGREDIENTS

- 1 small acorn squash
- 1 medium butternut squash
- 1 small to medium-sized apple
- 1 tsp coriander seeds
- 1 tsp cumin powder
- 1/8 tsp ground black pepper
- 1/2 tsp ground ginger
- 1/8 tsp ground cloves
- 1/4 tsp ground cinnamon
- 2 bay leaves
- Kosher salt
- 2 cans vegetable or chicken broth
- Dried parsley for garnish
- Non-stick cooking spray

DON'T HAVE AN APPLE?
Add a splash of apple juice.

CAN'T FIND AN ACORN SQUASH?
Use a large butternut and skip it.

SOUP TAKES TOO LONG?
Make it ahead and toast or warm the seeds just before serving.

ginger carrot soup with shrimp & rice

5 servings, 170 cals, 1g of fat, 4g of fiber.

INGREDIENTS

- 3 cups chicken or vegetable broth
- 1 bag of carrots (16 oz), peeled and chopped
- 1-1 1/2 inches of fresh ginger root, chopped
- About 1 cup water
- 2 cups cooked brown rice
- 6 oz cooked shrimp, chopped
- 2 green onions, chopped
- Dried parsley for garnish

STEPS

1. Over high heat, bring the broth, carrots and ginger to a boil. Continue to boil for about 10 minutes. Lower to a simmer and cook until carrots are tender, about 30 minutes.

2. Puree the cooked carrot mixture, either using a hand blender or transferring to a stand-alone blender. Return the puree to the pot.

3. Add 1 cup water (more if too thick), cooked rice, cooked shrimp and green onion. Bring back up to a boil then serve

COOKED SHRIMP?
Buy frozen cooked shrimp and defrost for quick stir-fries or soups like this!

DON'T LIKE SHRIMP?
Leftover chicken would work great!

NO CHICKEN?
Skip it or add some of your favorite beans!

This colorful soup is tasty, filling and wonderful at room temperature!

taco-ish soup with couscous & avocado

4 servings, 240 cals, 10g of fat, 10g of fiber.

INGREDIENTS

- 2 cups chicken broth or stock
- 1 (15 oz) can diced tomatoes
- 1 (15 oz) can kidney beans drained and rinsed
- 1 tsp chili powder
- 1 tsp garlic powder
- 1 tsp onion powder
- 1 tsp dried cilantro
- 1/2 tsp ground cumin
- 1/2 tbsp lime juice
- 2 oz (55g) whole wheat couscous
- 1 avocado, sliced
- 3/4 oz fancy shredded Mexican cheese blend

STEP

1. Place all the ingredients in a pot except avocado and cheese. Bring to a boil. Then cover and reduce to a simmer. **Simmer for about 10 minutes** or until couscous is soft.

2. **Scoop into 4 bowls,** top with avocado slices and a bit of the cheese.

DON'T LIKE AVOCADO?
Try a dollop of Greek yogurt.

CAN'T FIND COUSCOUS?
Brown rice or bulgar would be interesting.

LIKE A SOUPIER SOUP?
Double the broth.

Cooking out of the pantry can be quick and tasty. Add a touch of freshness with a ripe avocado & you have a quick, satisfying meal!

vegetable soup with leeks & kale

INGREDIENTS

- 1 tbsp olive oil (14g)
- 2 leeks, chopped
- 6 cloves garlic, minced
- 5 celery stalks with leaves, chopped
- 2-3 cups of carrots, chopped (around 300g)
- 1 cup of green and /or wax beans, cut in chunks
- 1 (15 oz) can white beans, drained and rinsed
- 4-5 sprigs fresh rosemary, stems removed and chopped
- About 7 cups of your favorite vegetable or chicken broth or stock
- About 1 lb fresh kale, stems removed and chopped

STEPS

1. **Heat the oil in a large stockpot** over medium heat. Add the leeks and garlic. Sauté until just soft. Add the celery, carrots and green beans, Stir to combine. Add the white beans and rosemary. Stir and continue to cook for a few minutes.

2. Add the broth and raise temperature to high to bring to just boiling. **Cover and lower to a simmer for about 30 minutes until the carrots soften.** Stir in the kale and cook for just a minute or two to soften or longer if desired. I like mine to still have some bite.

DON'T HAVE FRESH ROSEMARY?
Use about 1/4-1/2 tsp dried to taste.

WANT TO MAKE IT HEARTIER?
Add diced chicken!

DON'T LIKE KALE?
TRY IT! If you still don't like it, try spinach instead.

Soup is a great way to eat your vegetables, especially on a crisp fall day!

spiced tomato soup
with pinto beans

INGREDIENTS

- 1 can (10 3/4 oz) condensed tomato soup (preferably low sodium)
- 1 soup can of water
- 1 (15 oz) can diced tomatoes
- 1 (15 oz) can pinto beans, drained and rinsed
- 1 tsp chili powder
- 1 tsp dried cilantro
- 1/2 tsp cumin
- About 2 cups baby spinach, loosely chopped

STEPS

1. **Mix all ingredients except the spinach** in a pot over medium-high heat. Bring to a boil then lower the heat to medium and cook for 5 minutes allowing all the flavors to mix.

2. Turn off the heat. **Add the baby spinach** and remove from heat. Stir in the spinach. it will wilt in a few seconds. Serve.

3 servings, 240 cals, 2g of fat, 10g of fiber.

WANT EVEN MORE FLAVOR?
Buy diced tomatoes with green chili to kick it up a notch.

DON'T LIKE SPINACH?
Add some diced zucchini and bell pepper with the beans and tomatoes to up the vegetables.

LIKE IT REALLY SPICY?
Add some Tabasco or a diced up jalapeño in as well.

Sometimes you want a bowl of homemade soup but you just do not have the time. Why not get a little help in a can & turn something from your pantry into homemade-ish bowl of goodness.

GreenLiteBites

Sides

Servings vary, 27 cals, 3g of fiber.

NO LIMES?
Try lemon slices!

NO LEMONS?
How about an orange?

WANT EVEN MORE CITRUS FLAVOR?
Grate some of the lime peel before slicing.

STEPS

1. Preheat the oven to 375 degrees.

2. Line a cookie sheet with aluminum foil and spray with non-stick cooking spray.

3. Break off the ends of the asparagus, wash them and spread on the cookie sheet.

4. Season liberally with kosher salt. Top with lime slices.

5. Roast for 10-15 minutes shaking once or twice during cooking.

INGREDIENTS

- 1 bunch of asparagus, tough ends trimmed
- Kosher salt
- 1 lime, cut into thin slices
- Non-stick cooking spray

margarita
asparagus

Here's a twist on traditional roasted asparagus. Sometimes the simplest things make a tasty difference.

roasted cauliflower

About 4 servings, 50 cals, 1g of fat, 4g of fiber.

STEPS

1. **Preheat the oven** to 450 degrees.

2. **Cut and clean the cauliflower** and place in a large bowl.

3. **Mix the vinegar**, parsley, salt and pepper in a small bowl.

4. Pour the vinegar mixture over the cauliflower. **Toss to coat evenly** (a great job for the toddler, although we lost a few).

5. Spray a large cookie sheet with non-stick cooking spray. Pour the cauliflower and **spread them around the sheet.**

6. Roast for about 15 minutes, **shaking and tossing** a few times. After 15 minutes, sprinkle with the Parmesan cheese. Return to the oven for an additional 5 minutes.

7. Serve.

INGREDIENTS

- 1 head fresh cauliflower, cleaned and cut into bite-sized pieces
- 2 tbsp balsamic vinegar
- 1 tsp dried parsley
- Salt and pepper
- Non-stick cooking spray
- 1 tbsp Parmesan cheese

NO CAULIFLOWER?
Try this with broccoli!

OUT OF BALSAMIC?
How about a dash of soy sauce and Worcestershire?

LET THE KIDS HELP:
Put the cauliflower and spices in a big plastic bag and let them mix!

This idea converted my cauliflower-hating husband. He now loves it!

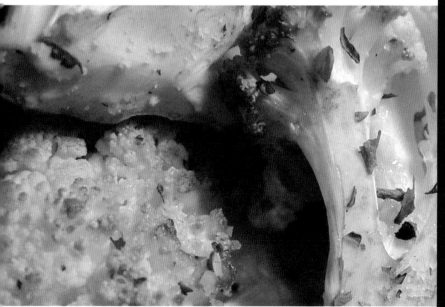

Why are appetizers usually breaded and deep fried? These stuffed mushrooms are a great alternative, Loaded with veggies and good for you!

simply stuffed mushrooms

STEPS

1. **Preheat the oven** to 400 degrees

2. **Clean the mushrooms** and remove stems. Mince the stems and set aside as they will be part of your stuffing.

3. **Mince the garlic**.

4. **Heat a small non-stick skillet** over medium heat, spray with cooking spray. Add the minced garlic and mushroom stems. Sprinkle with a bit of salt and pepper. While cooking, chop the spinach, you don't want large pieces or stems.

5. **Add the spinach** to the skillet a little at a time and cook down sprinkling a bit more salt and pepper.

6. **Remove filling from heat**. Line a cookie sheet with aluminum foil and spray with cooking spray. Stuff the mushrooms with the spinach mixture. Really jam it in there; you have more than enough.

7. **Top with Parmesan** cheese and bake for about 20 minutes

INGREDIENTS

- 8 oz package of white button mushrooms
- 3 large cloves of garlic, minced
- 4 cups of baby spinach leaves, chopped
- 2 tbsp (10g) Parmesan, shredded
- Kosher salt and pepper
- Olive oil cooking spray

WHEN TO MAKE?
Try these during the holidays on your guests. They'll never know how good they are for them.

TAKE TOO LONG?
Stuff ahead and make when ready to serve.

CHANGE IT UP A BIT!
Add some shallots or sweet onion to the stuffing.

About 4 servings, 190 cals, 0g of fat, 3g of fiber.

NO CREAM CHEESE?
A splash of skim milk works just fine.

NO BROTH?
Again, skim milk and a bit of extra salt.

WANT A MORE RUSTIC DISH?
Leave the skins on!

STEPS

1. **Peel and cut** the potatoes. Add them to a large pot filled with water (covering the potatoes by at least an inch) and cook over high heat until the potatoes are tender when forked. Note: time will depend on how small you cut the potatoes.

2. Drain the water.

3. Add cream cheese, broth and a pinch of salt and pepper. **Beat on high until desired consistency.** For "husband smooth," about 5 minutes.

INGREDIENTS

- About 4 large russet potatoes (2 lbs)
- 4 tbsp fat-free cream cheese (60g)
- 1/2 cup (4 oz) fat-free low-sodium chicken broth
- Pinch of kosher salt and pepper to taste

creamy mashed potatoes

You do not need butter and cream to make creamy mashed potatoes! Really! This recipe is a family favorite; we make it weekly and for all holidays.

delicata squash fries

STEPS

1. **Preheat** the oven to 425 degrees.

2. **Cut the squash in half** lengthwise and clean out the seeds with a spoon. Cut into long steak-fry chunks leaving the skin intact.

3. **Spray a cookie sheet** lined with aluminum foil with non-stick cooking spray. Layout the squash fries, spray with a bit more cooking spray and sprinkle with salt.

4. **Bake** for about 40 minutes, turning once.

INGREDIENTS

- 1 delicata squash
- Non-stick cooking spray
- Salt

This technique works great on just about any winter squash but the cute delicata is by far my favorite!

CAN'T FIND DELICATA?
Try a butternut or acorn squash.

DON'T THROW AWAY THE SEEDS!
Clean and roast them with some salt

MORE FLAVOR?
Try a sprinkle of your favorite spice. Cinnamon is a great complement!

cabbage feta salad

STEPS

1. **Whisk the feta,** honey, olive oil, oregano, vinegar, salt and pepper in a bowl, squishing the feta to make a creamy dressing.

2. **Pour the dressing** over the shredded cabbage. Toss.

This salad is coleslaw-like, but instead of mayonnaise it uses feta and some honey for great flavor and sweetness. It's a wonderful addition to any BBQ.

INGREDIENTS

- 1/4 cup crumbled feta (34g)
- 1/2 tbsp honey (10g)
- 1 tsp olive oil (5g)
- 1 tsp oregano
- 2 tbsp red wine vinegar
- Pinch of kosher salt and fresh-ground black pepper
- 1 small head of green cabbage, shredded (about 1 cup)
- 1 small head of red cabbage, shredded (about 1 cup)

CAN'T FIND RED CABBAGE?
That's OK, use only green!

CAN'T FIND GREEN?
Use only red!

HAVE FUN WITH IT!
Top your favorite burger, stuff it in a pita, add it to wraps.

slow cooker sweet potatoes

About 4 servings, 150 cals, 0g of fat, 4g of fiber.

STEPS

1. **Scrub the potatoes.** Cut into large chunks leaving skin on. Add them to the slow cooker.

2. In a small bowl, **whisk the honey,** molasses, vinegar and allspice to make the marinade.

3. **Pour the marinade** over the potatoes; stir to coat.

4. **Cover and cook** on high for about 4 hours, or low for 8, until potatoes are nice and soft.

5. Serve in a casserole dish with a **sprinkle of parsley.**

This is a great addition to holiday meals and has become a staple in my house. It's a favorite on Thanksgiving!

INGREDIENTS

- 4 large sweet potatoes (about 5 inches long)
- 1 tbsp honey (21g)
- 1 tbsp molasses (20g)
- 1 tbsp balsamic vinegar
- 1/4 tsp ground allspice
- Dried or fresh parsley for garnish

NOT ENOUGH FOR YOUR FAMILY?
Double or even triple the recipe! Just make sure it fits in your slow cooker!

MAKE IT YOUR OWN!
Add chunked carrots or other root veggies for a twist.

NO ALLSPICE?
A dash of nutmeg and/or cloves works great, too!

Dinner

Who says you need noodles to make lasagna! This recipe uses layers of zucchini and spaghetti squash creating a tasty, healthy meal.

zucchini & spaghetti squash lasagna

STEPS

1. **Preheat the oven** to 350 degrees.

2. In a casserole dish, **smear a little of the sauce** on the bottom to prevent sticking then begin layering zucchini, top with a bit of squash, dab on ricotta, sprinkle with a bit of the shredded cheese, add some sauce. Repeat until you are out of ingredients saving some of the mozzarella for the top.

3. **Sprinkle the top** with some ground pepper and dried parsley. Bake uncovered for at about 45 minutes until zucchini is tender.

4. During the baking process there will be a lot of water as there is no pasta to soak it up. About every 10-15 minutes **use a turkey baster to remove some excess water.**

5. **This recipe is even better double baked!** You can easily make it ahead and then pop it back in the oven. Just like traditional lasagna, it's better the next day!

INGREDIENTS

- About 2 cups red spaghetti sauce
- 1 medium zucchini, thinly sliced
- About 2-2 1/2 cups cooked spaghetti squash
- 1/2 cup fat-free ricotta cheese
- 3 oz fancy shredded mozzarella cheese
- Ground pepper
- Dried parsley

NEVER TRIED SPAGHETTI SQUASH?

Try it! 15 minutes in the microwave and you have a healthy pasta alternative.

CAN'T FIND FAT-FREE RICOTTA?

Try the part skim variety.

WHAT'S FANCY SHREDDED CHEESE?

It's shredded finer allowing you to stretch it a bit further.

sausage & pepper skewers

STEPS

1. Preheat the grill.

2. Put the olive oil, vinegar and Italian seasoning in a large bowl. Add the pepper and onion chunks. Toss in the oil mixture to coat.

3. Cut each sausage link into 4-5 chunks. If you keep the sausage slightly frozen, this is much easier. Simply defrost frozen sausage for a few minutes in the microwave.

4. Toss the sausage chunks with the peppers and onions.

5. Skewer the sausage with the pepper and onion, alternating the three ingredients.

6. Make 8 skewers.

7. Lower the grill to medium and cook for 20-25 minutes, turning frequently.

INGREDIENTS

- 1 tsp olive oil
- 1 tsp white vinegar
- 1 tsp Italian seasoning
- 1 large green bell pepper, cut into large chunks
- 1 large red pepper, cut into large chunks
- 2 thick slices of a large sweet onion, cut into large chunks
- 20 oz (6) Italian turkey sausage links
- 8 skewer sticks
- Non-stick cooking spray (for grill)

Sausage and peppers are just made to be eaten together. This simple idea takes the classic combo out to the grill in a fun way!

NO GRILL?
Place the skewers under the broiler!

BULK IT UP!
Add even more veggies. Broccoli, mushrooms and zucchini chunks work great!

HOW TO SHOW?
Place the skewers on top of a bed of brown rice for a pretty presentation.

mojito
tilapia

STEPS

1. Whisk the lemon and lime juice, zest, honey and mint leaves together. Sprinkle both sides of the tilapia with a bit of kosher salt. Pour the lime juice mixture over the tilapia fillets and marinate for about an hour.

2. Spray a non-stick frying pan with cooking spray and place over medium-high heat. Cook for about 3 minutes a side until fish flakes with a fork.

INGREDIENTS

- Juice of 1 lemon
- Juice of 2 limes
- Zest of one of the limes
- 1 tbsp honey
- About 1 tbsp fresh mint leaves, chopped (save a few to garnish)
- 4-6 tilapia fillets, about 4 oz each
- Kosher salt

A Mojito is a Cuban drink flavored with fresh lime & mint leaves - two flavors that I happen to think also go great with fish!

NO FRESH LIMES?
Substitute with 3 tbsp lime juice and 1 lemon.

CAN'T FIND FRESH MINT?
Use a teaspoon of dried.

TRY A DIFFERENT FISH!
How about cod, snapper or orange roughy?

This is a husband favorite! We serve it over mashed potatoes or whole wheat noodles and pair it with our favorite green veggies.

About 4 servings, 175 cals, 3g of fat, 2g of fiber.

NOT THICK ENOUGH?

Add another tablespoon of whole wheat flour mixed with a quarter cup of water and bring back up to a boil.

NOT INTO PORK?

This recipe works great with boneless chicken breasts as well!

SERVE WITH?

Goes great with Creamy Mashed Potatoes and the vegetable of your choice!

STEPS

1. If the chops are thick, lay them on a sheet of plastic wrap. **Top with another sheet and bang away** until the pork is 1/4-1/2 inch thick.

2. **Heat a large skillet over medium-high heat** and spray with non-stick spray. Season both sides of the pork with a bit of salt and pepper. Once the pan is hot, add the chops. Don't crowd the pan, do them in batches if you have to. Flip after 2-3 minutes and cook for another 2-3 minutes.

3. **Remove the pork** from the skillet and set aside.

4. Lower the heat to medium and spray the skillet with a bit more spray and add the onion. **Stir and add the mushrooms and garlic.** Add the apple cider vinegar. Stir.

5. While the mushrooms are cooking, **whisk the broth,** Worcestershire sauce and flour. Add to the pan and bring to a boil. Put the chops back in and simmer for 5-10 minutes until ready to serve.

INGREDIENTS

- 4 boneless pork loin chops, about 4 oz each
- Kosher salt and pepper
- 1/2 sweet onion, diced
- 10 oz package of mushrooms, sliced
- 3 cloves of garlic, minced
- 1 tbsp apple cider vinegar or applesauce
- 1 cup of your favorite broth (chicken, beef, vegetable)
- 1 tbsp Worcestershire sauce
- 1 tbsp whole wheat flour
- Non-stick cooking spray

pork chops with simple mushroom gravy

easy slow cooker vegetarian chili

About 8 servings, 300 cals, 3g of fat, 10g of fiber.

STEPS

1. **Put all ingredients in the slow cooker,** stir and cook on low for 5 hours or 3 hours on high.

INGREDIENTS

- 1 can black beans, drained and rinsed
- 1 can kidney beans, drained and rinsed
- 1 can chickpeas, drained and rinsed
- 1 can corn, undrained
- 1 can diced tomatoes with green chilies
- 1 small can (6oz) tomato paste
- 1 bell pepper, chopped
- 1 small onion, diced
- 1/2 tbsp chili powder
- 1/2 tbsp ground cumin
- 1 tbsp dried cilantro

TOO SPICY?
Replace the diced tomatoes with green chili with plain diced tomatoes.

NOT SPICY ENOUGH?
Add Tabasco or red pepper flakes or chopped jalapeños

DONT HAVE THE SAME BEANS?
Try pinto, Northern or pink!

This takes advantage of your slow cooker and raids the pantry to make a tasty dinner when you just don't have time to babysit the stove.

When I serve this with creamy mashed potatoes, the husband always gives me a big smile. Little does he know it takes about 10 minutes to make.

simple chicken tips with gravy

STEPS

1. **Heat a skillet** over medium-high heat and spray with non-stick cooking spray. Add the onion.

   Sprinkle with kosher salt and pepper and cook until browned. Add the cut chicken. It may stick; just leave it for a minute to give it a sear then toss in the pan a few times.

2. Once the chicken is browned, **pile it in the middle of the pan**. Pour the cream of chicken soup on top. Fill the can about three-quarters full with water.

   Give it a stir to get the soup that stuck and pour it in the skillet. Stir until dissolved. Stir in the Worcestershire sauce, coffee powder and browning agent. Bring to a boil then cover and lower to a simmer until ready to serve.

INGREDIENTS

- Non-stick cooking spray
- Kosher salt and pepper
- 1 small sweet onion, diced
- 2 boneless chicken breasts with all visible fat removed and cut into chunks (about 1 lb)
- 1 (10 3/4 oz) can fat-free cream of chicken soup
- 1 tbsp Worcestershire sauce
- 1 tsp instant coffee powder
- 1/2 tsp Gravy Master or other browning agent

NO INSTANT COFFEE?
Use a splash of brewed.

CAN'T FIND A BROWNING AGENT?
Use a teaspoon of molasses.

HAVE FRESH HERBS?
A bit of thyme goes wonderfully in this.

quick quinoa &turkey taco stew

About 6 servings, 250 cals, 4g of fat, 7g of fiber.

STEPS

1. **In a large pot** sprayed with non-stick cooking spray, brown the ground turkey and onion over medium heat.

2. Add the zucchini, peppers and taco seasoning. **Stir to coat** all the vegetables with the seasoning.

3. Add the beans, diced tomatoes, broth and quinoa. Turn the heat to high and bring to a boil. Then cover and **simmer about 20** minutes until quinoa soaks up most of the liquid.

4. **Stir in the lime juice** and serve. I sprinkle a bit of shredded Mexican cheese blend on top.

Quinoa adds a fun texture to this one-pot tasty meal.

INGREDIENTS

- 8 oz 99% lean ground turkey
- 1 small onion, diced
- 1 medium zucchini, chopped
- 1 small sweet pepper, chopped (red, orange or yellow)
- 1 package of taco seasoning (preferably low sodium)
- 1 (15 oz) can pinto beans drained and rinsed
- 1 (15 oz) can of diced tomatoes with chilies
- 1 (14 oz) can of broth (chicken, beef or vegetable)
- 1 cup (170 g) quinoa
- 1 tbsp lime juice
- Non-stick cooking spray
- Shredded Mexican cheese blend (optional)

NEW TO QUINOA?
This is a great starter dish! It's healthy and cooks up fast!

CAN'T FIND QUINOA?
Try whole wheat couscous or brown rice.

NO TACO SEASONING?
Try a combination of chili powder, cumin, garlic and salt.

baked ham with sweet potatoes & carrots

Servings and nutritional Information will vary based on size of the ham.

NO ALLSPICE?
Try nutmeg or a dash of cloves

BULK IT UP!
Add more root vegetables such as parsnips and/or turnips.

NO CORNSTARCH?
Try a little whole wheat flour as a thickener.

INGREDIENTS

- 1 small cured ham
- Handful of whole cloves (optional)
- 1 large sweet potato, cut in small chunks
- 3/4 cup baby carrots, cut in half
- 1 tbsp apple cider vinegar
- 1 tbsp balsamic vinegar
- 1 tbsp (21g) honey
- 1 tbsp (20g) molasses
- 1/4 tsp allspice
- 1/2 cup water (separated)
- 1/2 tbsp cornstarch

A small baked ham is a great, lean meat option for dinner. Pair with some root vegetables and a simple sweet glaze for a complete meal!

STEPS

1. **Preheat the oven** to 375 degrees.

2. **Insert cloves** in the flesh of the ham to add flavor.

3. **Place the ham in a baking dish** and spread the sweet potato and carrots around it.

4. In a small bowl whisk the apple cider vinegar, balsamic vinegar, honey, molasses, allspice and 1/4 cup of the water. **Pour over the ham**, potatoes and carrots.

5. Cover the baking dish with aluminum foil and **bake for an hour** until potatoes are soft.

6. Whisk the cornstarch with remaining 1/4 cup of water. When finished, remove the ham, potatoes and carrots from the baking dish. **Place the dish over medium heat**, add the cornstarch mixture and continue to stir while bringing it to a boil, allowing the sauce to thicken to a glaze.

7. Top the ham with a **bit of the glaze** and serve with a side of potatoes and carrots.

Ahi tuna is a special treat in our house. When it goes on sale you can bet I'm the first one in line.

blackened ahi tuna with simple mango salsa

INGREDIENTS

SIMPLE MANGO SALSA
- 1/2 mango, diced
- 1-2 slices onion, diced (red or Vidalia)
- 10-15 grape tomatoes, halved
- 1/2 tsp dried cilantro
- 1 tsp lime juice

TUNA
- 1/2 tsp each: onion powder, garlic powder, chili powder, paprika
- 1/4 tsp each: cumin, oregano, basil, black pepper
- 1/8 tsp each: ground red pepper, kosher salt
- Non-stick cooking spray
- 2 ahi tuna steaks (aka yellowfin), 4oz each

STEPS

1. Mix all the ingredients for the mango salsa and set aside.

2. Mix all the blackening spices together.

3. Heat a skillet over high heat. Spray with non-stick cooking spray.

4. Dip one side of the tuna into the spices and immediately place on the skillet, spice side down. Repeat with the other fillet. Cook for 3 minutes.

5. Remove the tuna from heat and dip the other sides in the spices and place back into the skillet. Cook for an additional 2-3 minutes.

6. Remove from the heat and top with the salsa.

TUNA BREAKING THE BANK?
Try this with tilapia or cod.

NO MANGO?
Try pineapple, melon or even strawberries!

TOO MANY SPICES?
Go for a simpler combination of garlic and chili powders with the salt and pepper.

baked parmesan breaded tilapia

INGREDIENTS

- 1/2 cup (30g) high-fiber cereal
- 1/4 cup (20g) Parmesan cheese
- 1/2 tsp onion powder
- 1/2 tsp garlic powder
- 1 tsp Italian seasoning
- 4-6 tilapia fillets
- Salt and pepper
- Non-stick cooking spray

STEPS

1. **Preheat** the broiler.

2. **Place the cereal**, Parmesan cheese and spices in a blender or food processor to make the breading.

3. Season the fish with salt and pepper. **Dip the fillets** in breading to coat.

4. Spray a cookie sheet lined with aluminum foil with non-stick cooking spray, **place fillets on sheet and spray tops** with cooking spray.

5. **Broil the fish** 2 racks from the top for about 3-4 minutes a side.

Who says breading has to be made with bread! Try some Fiber One, All-Bran, Grape-Nuts or even shredded wheat for this simple dish.

NO BROILER?
Bake in a 400-degree oven about 6 minutes a side.

SPICE IT UP?
Dip the fillets in Tabasco and add a bit of cayenne to the breading.

SERVE WITH:
My favorite, sweet potato fries and peas!

1 serving, 200 cals, 9g of fat, 16g of fiber.

Skillet veggies are a favorite of mine. They are quick, tasty, healthy and happen to make great tacos!

WANT TO UP THE PROTEIN?
Add some black beans or cooked chicken.

NOT A FETA FAN?
Try some shredded cheddar.

COOKING FOR MORE THAN ONE?
Grab a big skillet and quadruple the recipe!

STEPS

1. **Heat a small non-stick skillet** over medium-high heat. Spray with non-stick cooking spray.

2. **Add the onion** and leave it alone for about 2 minutes, allowing the onion to brown.

3. Toss the onion and then **add the remaining veggies.**

4. Sprinkle with a bit of kosher salt and pepper. **Toss to coat everything,** cover and cook for 2 minutes.

5. After 2 minutes uncover, **add the basil and oregano.** Toss to coat everything and cover again for 2 more minutes.

6. Warm the shells either in a skillet or in the microwave for a few seconds. Split the veggie filling between the two shells. **Top with the feta** and a dash of hot sauce.

INGREDIENTS

- Non-stick cooking spray
- 2 slices sweet onion, chopped
- About 1/4 cup zucchini, chopped
- About 1/4 cup yellow squash, chopped
- About 1/4 cup bell pepper, chopped
- 8 grape tomatoes, halved
- Kosher salt
- Black pepper
- 1/2 tsp dried basil
- 1 tsp dried oregano
- 2 small whole wheat taco shells
- 1 oz crumbled feta
- Green chili or Tabasco sauce

skillet veggie & feta tacos for one

vegged-out
sloppy joes

INGREDIENTS

- 20 oz lean ground beef (at least 90% lean)
- 20 oz lean ground turkey (at least 90% lean)
- 1 large Vidalia onion, diced
- 3 stalks celery, diced
- 1 medium zucchini, diced
- 2 green peppers, diced
- 1/2 bag baby spinach, chopped
- 1 (15.5 oz) can sloppy Joe sauce
- 1 (15 oz) can diced tomatoes
- 1 (6 oz) can tomato paste

STEPS

1. Brown the meats with the onion and all the veggies. I start with the meats and onion in a large stock pot and then cut the veggies in **order, adding them and stirring them in the pot.**

2. Transfer the browned meat and veggies to a slow cooker, **add the sloppy Joe sauce,** tomatoes and paste. Cook on high 2 hours or low for 4.

3. Serve with a variety of buns.

NO SLOW COOKER?
Keep everything in the stock pot and simmer on low for 2-4 hours.

NO BUNS?
Serve over brown rice or even whole wheat pasta!

MORE VEGGIES?
Try diced carrots, summer squash and multicolor peppers!

Make this for your next party, and no one will know it's healthy and loaded with fresh vegetables!

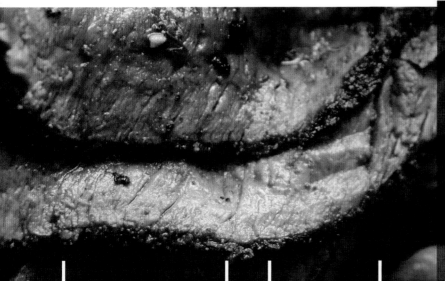

About 5 servings, 160 cals, 7g of fat, 0g of fiber.

SERVE WITH?
Corn on the cob and quick sugar snap peas warmed in the skillet.

LEFTOVERS?
Use thin cuts to make cheesesteaks for another tasty meal!

HAVE A GRILL?
Cook this baby outside!

dry-rubbed pan-fried london broil

INGREDIENTS

- About a pound of choice beef about 1-inch thick
- 1/2 tsp kosher salt
- 1/2 tsp fresh ground black pepper
- 1 tsp garlic powder
- 1 tsp onion powder
- 1/2 tsp chili powder
- 1/2 tsp ground cumin

Simple yet delicious! This dry rub uses stock pantry items to transform a simple London broil into a tasty family pleaser.

STEPS

1. **Pull the defrosted London broil out** of the fridge an hour or two before dinner. A room-temperature steak cooks better.

2. **Make the dry rub** by mixing spices together. Sprinkle the rub on both sides of the beef using all of it.

3. Heat a skillet over medium-high heat. Make sure it is nice and hot and then **add the steak.**

4. **Cook** it for 4-5 minutes then flip.

5. Cook for an **additional 4-5 minutes.**

6. Remove from the skillet and **let rest for at least 10 minutes** for medium-rare. For medium-well, transfer the meat to a preheated 350-degree oven to finish cooking.

7. **Cut the beef against the grain** so that you can see lines up and down the cuts.

What happens when you combine the concept of a pot pie with the flavors of your favorite Mexican restaurant? This fun, fabulous dinner!

THE CRUST

INGREDIENTS

- 1/4 cup (~22g) whole wheat pastry flour
- 1/4 cup (30 g) cornmeal
- 1 tsp baking soda
- Pinch of salt
- 1 tsp (5g) molasses
- 1 egg white
- 2 oz milk
- Non-stick cooking spray

STEPS

1. **Preheat the oven** to 350 degrees.

2. **Mix the flour,** cornmeal, baking soda and salt together. Add the rest of the ingredients and whisk well.

3. **Pour the batter** into a standard pie pan. You may have to tilt and twist the pan around until batter is distributed evenly.

4. **Bake for about 10 minutes** until firm to the touch.

mexican pie

INGREDIENTS

THE FILLING

- 1 small sweet onion, chopped
- 8 oz extra-lean ground turkey (99% lean preferred)
- 1 tsp chili powder
- 1 tsp dried cilantro
- 1/2 tsp cumin
- 1 bell pepper, chopped

- 1 jalapeño, seeded and diced
- 1 medium tomato, seeded and chopped
- 1 (16 oz) can fat-free refried beans
- 1/2 cup salsa
- 1 oz fancy shredded Mexican cheese blend
- Non-stick cooking spray

STEPS

1. **Heat a large non-stick skillet** over medium heat and sweat the onion with a bit of non-stick cooking spray. Add the ground turkey and brown.

2. **Once the turkey is cooked** (all white), add the chili powder, cilantro and cumin. Stir in the chopped peppers, jalapeño and tomatoes. Continue cooking over medium heat for a few minutes allowing all flavors to combine.

3. In a large bowl, **mix the refried beans** and skillet mixture. Combine all ingredients well.

4. Pour the filling in the pie pan with the crust. Pack it down and **smear the salsa on top**. Sprinkle with cheese.

5. **Bake** in the preheated 350-degree oven for about 20 minutes.

6. **Let set for about 5 minutes** before removing a slice.

   It holds together a bit better.

WANT IT SPICIER?
Leave the seeds in the jalapeño and/or add a dash of Tabasco.

MORE COLOR?
Mix it up by using red, yellow and orange bell peppers.

NO TIME?
Make the pie ahead and bake when ready to eat.

GreenLiteBites

Sweets

black & blue dessert cups

STEPS

1. **Preheat** oven to 375 degrees.

2. **Mix the berries** and honey.

3. Place the wonton wrappers in a mini-muffin pan, forming little cups. **Evenly distribute the berry** mixture among the cups.

4. **Bake** for 10 minutes.

5. Remove from oven, let cool a bit then **dust with powdered sugar** and garnish with a mint leaf.

INGREDIENTS

- 1/2 cup blackberries (74g)
- 1/2 cup blueberries (72g)
- 1 tbsp honey (21g)
- 8 small wonton wrappers
- Dusting of powdered sugar (1/8 tsp)
- 8 fresh mint leaves for garnish

I love simple, light, tasty desserts. These are fun little cups bursting with fresh fruit and a touch of honey. They are a great way to end a meal or satisfy a sweet craving!

NOT A BLACKBERRY FAN?
Try raspberries!

CHANGE IT UP!
Add some peaches and a dash of cinnamon!

DINNER PARTY?
Double or triple the batch for a fun, light dessert!

72

chocolate
ricotta rolls

About 2 servings, 110 cals, 1g of fat, 2g of fiber.

INGREDIENTS

- 6 wonton wrappers
- 1/2 cup fat-free ricotta cheese (124g)
- 1/4 - 1/2 tsp stevia powder
  (or other sweetener to your tasting)
- 1/4 tsp cinnamon
- 1/2 tsp cocoa powder
- 1/4 tsp vanilla extract
- Dusting of cocoa powder, stevia or powdered
  sugar for dusting

STEPS

1. **Preheat the oven** to 350 degrees.

2. **Roll the wrappers into tube** shapes sealing with a bit of
   water. Stand them upright on a cookie sheet and bake for 10-
   12 minutes.

3. **Mix the ricotta cheese**, stevia, cinnamon and cocoa powder.

4. Plop the **cheese mixture** in a sealable plastic bag, snip off
   the corner and squeeze out to fill wonton tubes.

5. **Dust with cocoa** powder and stevia.

OUT OF VANILLA EXTRACT?
Try a dash of almond for a fun twist!

CHOCOLATE NUT?
Add a handful of mini-chocolate chips.

ANOTHER TWIST:
Swap out the vanilla for a raspberry extract,
up the cocoa and add the chips!

Wonton wrappers are
such fun little vessels!
Here's a fun idea turning
savory ricotta into a
sweet dessert.

dried fruit & whole wheat walnut oatmeal cookies

About 18 servings (2 cookies ea.), 96 cals, 3g of fat, 1g of fiber.

INGREDIENTS

- 1 cup white whole wheat flour (120g)
- 1 cup old fashioned oats (80g)
- 3/4 teaspoon baking powder
- 1/2 teaspoon baking soda
- 1/2 teaspoon salt
- 1/2 cup raw sugar (105g)
- 1 tbsp molasses (20g)

- 2 tbsp butter
- 2 oz fat-free cream cheese
- 1 1/2 teaspoons vanilla extract
- 1 large egg
- 1/4 cup chopped walnuts, toasted (30g)
- 1/3 cup raisins or dried fruit, chopped (I use a combo of cherries and blueberries)

With walnuts & dried fruit, these are a great addition to any cookie swap.

STEPS

1. **Preheat** oven to 350 degrees.

2. **Combine flour**, oats, baking powder, baking soda and salt. Set aside.

3. Place the sugar, molasses, butter and cream cheese in a bowl and beat with a mixer at medium-high speed until well blended. **Add vanilla and egg** beat again until blended.

4. **Gradually add the flour-oat mixture** to the wet ingredients, beating at low speed just until combined. Once all the dry ingredients are incorporated, stir in walnuts and dried fruit.

5. **Drop dough** by tablespoonfuls onto baking sheets sprayed with non-stick cooking spray or lined with parchment paper. The dough will be sticky; try to flatten a bit as the dough will not melt as much as traditional cookies. Make 36 cookies (3 dozen).

6. **Bake at 350 degrees** for 12 minutes or until edges of cookies are lightly browned. Cool on the cookie sheet for at least 2 minutes.

NO WALNUTS?
Try almonds and dried cherries.

NOT A NUT PERSON?
Add a handful of mini chocolate chips.

LIKE CHOCOLATE COOKIES?
Try Chocolate Oatmeal Walnut Cookies recipe on GreenLiteBites.com.

chocolate cookie crisps

STEPS

1. **Preheat** the oven to 350 degrees.

2. **Mix** the flour, cocoa powder, baking soda and salt and set aside.

3. Melt the butter, chocoate chips and molasses over very low heat or in a double boiler, **stirring contstantly.**

4. Once the chips and butter are melted, remove from heat. **Start beating the chocolate mixture on low**, adding the cream cheese and egg. Beat for about 2 minutes until smooth, although you will see some white specks from the cheese. Continue to beat, slowly adding the flour mixture. Once the flour is incorporated, the dough will be thick and sticky.

5. Take half the dough and place it on parchment paper, top with another sheet and roll out to 1/4 inch or less. **The thinner you roll, the crisper the cookie.**

6. **Remove the first dough** from the freezer, peel away top paper and cut using your favorite cookie cutters.

7. **Place on cookie sheet** and bake for 8-10 minutes. Makes about 40 cookies.

INGREDIENTS

- 1 cup (120g) whole wheat flour
- 1/4 cup (20g) unsweetened cocoa powder
- 1/2 tsp baking soda
- 1/4 tsp salt
- 2 tbsp butter
- 4 oz semisweet chocolate chips
- 1 tbsp (20g) molasses
- 1 oz fat-free cream cheese
- 1 egg

About 13 servings, 105 cals, 4g of fat, 2g of fiber.

Crispy chocolate cookies, need I say more?

IN A FESTIVE MOOD?
Add sprinkles before baking.

NO COOKIE CUTTERS?
Roll dough and squish with a fork to make a pattern.

OUT OF TIME?
Roll the dough and store in the fridge until ready.

Fruit makes the best dessert! It's naturally sweet and full of natural goodness.

raspberry stuffed
peaches

STEPS

1. Preheat the oven to 425 degrees.

2. Wash and halve the peaches, removing the pit. The easiest way to do this is to cut around the perimeter and twist apart. Then simply scrape out the pulp and pit with a spoon so you have 6 halves.

3. Mix the cereal, oats and cinnamon together. Combine the honey, oat mixture and raspberries, mixing well.

4. Scoop the raspberry-oat mixture two raspberries at a time and press into the center of each peach half.

5. Bake for 15 minutes until soft.

INGREDIENTS

- 3 fresh peaches
- 1/8 cup crunchy Grape-Nut-like cereal (14g)
- 1/8 cup old fashioned rolled oats (10g)
- 1/4 tsp cinnamon
- 1 tbsp honey
- 1/2 cup fresh raspberries (61g)

NOT A RASPBERRY PERSON?
Try blueberries or blackberries.

IN THE MOOD FOR ICE CREAM?
Add a scoop of vanilla yogurt!

NO HONEY?
Try agave or even maple syrup!

STEPS

1. **Pop the popcorn** in the microwave according to instructions.

2. In a large stock pot, **melt the honey and chocolate** over very low heat. Stir frequently to combine.

3. Slowly **add the popcorn** to the pot & stir to coat until all popcorn is added.

INGREDIENTS

- 1 bag of 94% fat-free popcorn, popped
- 1 tbsp honey (21g)
- 1/4 square of unsweetened baking chocolate (3.5g)

About 4 servings, 105 cals, 3g of fat, 2g of fiber.

quick chocolate kettlecorn

NO HONEY?
Try agave nectar.

NO UNSWEETENED CHOCOLATE?
Use a few dark chocolate squares and skip the honey.

MORE OF A CINNAMON PERSON?
Don't melt anything and simply sprinkle with cinnamon and your favorite sweetener.

Next time you have a chocolate craving, try this quick trick to transform a bag of microwave popcorn.

grilled chocolate & cherries

STEPS

1. **Separate the sandwich** thin in half and spread the mini chips on one side.

2. Place the halved cherries **on top of the chips**. Replace the top.

3. Heat a skillet over medium-high heat. Spray with non-stick cooking spray. **Transfer the thin to the skillet.** Cook for 1 minute, pressing with a spatula or smaller pan.

4. **Flip and cook** for an additional minute while pressing it down a bit.

INGREDIENTS

- 1 whole-grain sandwich thin
- 1 tbsp mini chocolate chips (14g)
- 1 oz fresh cherries (28g about 5), pitted and halved
- Non-stick cooking spray

NO CHERRIES?
Try this with blueberries.

NO BERRIES?
How about a banana?

NO SANDWICH THIN?
Try a slice of whole grain bread or a tortilla.

This is a great idea for those days you want dessert but just don't have the time or desire to bake.

Notes:

_____   _____

_____   _____

_____   _____

_____   _____

_____   _____

_____   _____

_____   _____

_____   _____

_____   _____

_____   _____

_____   _____

_____   _____

_____   Thanks for reading!
                                                    -Roni
_____

Made in the USA
Charleston, SC
25 March 2011